"Intimate and m from the heart of Scripture is evident ~~ ~~, ~~ , itations that draw you into a deeper relationship with Christ."
MOST REVEREND STEPHEN D. PARKES, DD, *Bishop of Savannah*

"This book caught me off guard in the best way possible, with an authentic, plain-spoken depth that makes spirituality as real as the breath in my lungs. The authentic, compassionate language touched my heart when it needed touching, comforted my spirit when it needed comforting, and challenged my thinking when it needed challenging."
S. JAMES MEYER, *author of Jesus Wears Socks with Sandals and God Plays a Purple Banjo*

"I've always been drawn to books that help to bring alive the words of Jesus. Suddenly, Jesus is in the room and speaking directly to me. *Heart-to-Heart Talks with Jesus* delivers in a big way. I look forward to spending time in prayer with this valuable resource!"
GARY ZIMAK, *bestselling author, speaker, and radio host*

"Beautiful! Inspiring! Easy to read yet profound in thought!"
BISHOP SAMUEL JACOBS, *bishop-emeritus of the Diocese of Houma-Thibodaux*

"Deacons Ensley and Herrmann have written a wonderful devotional in the tradition of *The Imitation of Christ*. Avoiding any saccharine devotion, they find the delicate balance of personal devotion and solid theological grounding."
JOHN MICHAEL TALBOT, *composer and spiritual writer, founder of the Inner Room School of Spirituality*

"*Heart-to-Heart Talks with Jesus* could not have arrived at a better time. It picked me up out of my anxiety, my sleepless nights. The imagined words of Jesus in this book touched my heart and soothed my soul."

JUDY ESWAY, *author of Real Life, Real Spirituality*

"A helpful guide on many levels:
- » one who is beginning to pray in one's own words will find mentoring;
- » one who is seeking healing will experience the touch of Jesus;
- » one who is grieving will receive the gentle outreach of compassion;
- » one who is growing will be challenged to become the gospel carrier;
- » everyone will sense that Jesus of the Scripture is Jesus of our lives."

SR. MARY ANNE SCHAENZER, SSND, *editor of Pentecost Today*

"While reading *Heart-to-Heart Talks with Jesus*, I was instantly reconnected to God's love—a love that is tender, vast, creative, unending, patient, forgiving, challenging, and exuberant. Rooted in nature and Scripture, it offers a much-needed message for our times."

MELANNIE SVOBODA, SND, *author of The Grace of Beauty: Its Mystery, Power, and Delight in Daily Life*

"*Heart-to-Heart Talks with Jesus* is a multilayered work of art. Each message manifests the authors' deep knowledge of not only the written word of Scripture but also and more importantly the Word made Flesh, Jesus Christ."

REV. DOUGLAS K. CLARK, STL, *theological advisor to the bishop of Savannah and censor librorum*

"I recommend this book to anyone who wants to have a deeper and more personal relationship with the Lord. It is awesome!"

RICHARD GENE ARNO, PHD, *founder, The National Christian Counselors Assn.*

Heart-to-Heart Talks with Jesus

INTIMATE ENCOUNTERS WITH OUR LOVING SAVIOR

DEACON EDDIE ENSLEY
and DEACON ROBERT HERRMANN

TWENTY-THIRD PUBLICATIONS
One Montauk Avenue, Suite 200
New London, CT 06320
(860) 437-3012 or (800) 321-0411
www.twentythirdpublications.com

Copyright © 2021 Deacon Eddie Ensley and Deacon Robert Herrmann. All rights reserved. No part of this publication may be reproduced in any manner without prior written permission of the publisher. Write to the Permissions Editor.

Cover photo: © Shutterstock.com / CURAphotography

ISBN: 978-1-62785-599-0
Printed in the U.S.A.

A division of Bayard, Inc.

Contents

vii	FOREWORD
1	INTRODUCTION
5	**Feel the Lord's Love**
27	REFLECTION QUESTIONS
29	**Learn about the Lord**
57	REFLECTION QUESTIONS
59	**Take Comfort in the Lord**
81	REFLECTION QUESTIONS
83	**Feel Amazement in the Lord's Presence**
102	REFLECTION QUESTIONS

*I dedicate this book to
my spiritual friend, Dr. Ivy Mallisham,
whose encouragement help make
this book possible.*

*And to my living first cousins
whom I hold dear in my heart:
Margie Hale, Philip Crittenden,
Randy Crittenden, Beverly Lang,
and Gary Pearson and
my almost first cousin, Elaine Klepac*

*Many thanks to the superb job
my private editor, Patrice Fagnant MacArthur,
did in helping craft this book, especially her help
with the prayers and reflections*

Foreword

I first met Eddie Ensley briefly in 1977, shortly after he had written *Sounds of Wonder*, a historical and timely study on the gifts of the Spirit. It was full of much-needed understanding and wisdom at a time when the gifts were being poured out in abundance upon Catholics and all Christians alike.

It wasn't until around 2014 that I would meet Eddie again, but Eddie was no stranger to me. I had been reading his books during this thirty-five-year span and felt like I knew Eddie as a close friend. His style of writing is extremely vulnerable and intimate. One cannot read his works without coming to know this man of God in a deep way. And one cannot read his works without coming to know God in a much more profound and intimate way. *Heart-to-Heart Talks with Jesus: Intimate Encounters with Our Loving Savior* is no exception. At a time when the Covid pandemic and social unrest can leave us unsettled and full of fear, these messages from the Lord provide reassurance and peace—knowing his love is ever surrounding us and carrying us.

Eddie has made known through his books the incredible story of his life. It is even painful to read some of the incidents and struggles he faced as a child and while growing up. But he chose the "narrow way." Rather than use his struggles and obstacles to blame God or run from God, Eddie chose to press into God, deeper and deeper. The result is an intimacy with God and an exceptional ability to hear the voice of God in prayer. "I know my own and my own know me" (Jn 10:14).

Deacon Robert Herrmann, the assistant author, holds a similar spirituality to Eddie's and played a major role in crafting and shaping the messages.

There are some who would ask the question, "How can we know these messages are from God?" It's a good question because we are to test all "prophecy" (I Thes 5:19–21). There is no guarantee. However, Matthew 7:16 also applies: "You shall know them by their fruits." As someone who has been privileged to be part of Deacon Eddie's spiritual direction journey, the fruit is manifest in his life and in these messages: love, peace, joy, forgiveness, patient endurance, mercy, kindness, self-control. These fruits the Enemy cannot imitate.

I would encourage readers to allow these messages to speak to your heart. In doing so, perhaps you also will hear the loving, consoling, and challenging voice of the Lord in your own life, bringing about a subtle but real transformation.

DAN ALMETER
SEPTEMBER 23, 2020, FEASTDAY OF PADRE PIO

Dan Almeter, LPC, serves as Deacon Eddie Ensley's spiritual director. He is a pastoral leader in the Alleluia Community where he coordinates the Alleluia School of Spiritual Direction.

Introduction

What would it be like to have a heart-to-heart talk with Jesus himself? What would Jesus tell you? What would you tell him?

In unsettled times it is natural to seek deep assurance. God's intimate presence provides that assurance. When things are uncertain, we seek the immediate nearness of God, not just ideas about God. We want to be drawn into life-changing intimacy with God.

The daily devotionals in *Heart-to-Heart Talks with Jesus: Intimate Encounters with Our Loving Savior* can help lead you and those you love to that holy embrace. Written in the form of God speaking to you as to his loved and treasured child, these devotionals can reveal the nature of his love more clearly in its depth, its splendor, and its tenderness. Full of practical advice and comfort, these messages lead you to a life-enhancing communion with God.

It may seem presumptuous to write in a form that has messages from Jesus directly to you, yet this form of devotional is classic and has long been acknowledged and respected in the Catholic Church. *The Imitation of Christ* by Thomas à Kempis and many other classics of Catholic spirituality were written in this style.

For several decades I have used this form of devotional writing in my private devotional life, as has Deacon Robert Herrmann. I pray in front of an Icon Wall with one of the icons being the St. Catherine icon of Christ from St. Catherine Monastery at Mount Sinai. In writing *Heart-to-Heart Talks with Jesus*, I would read the Scriptures for long periods of time plus classic and modern spiritual literature, letting it seed my subconscious, letting the message and inspiration sink deep within. I would look at the St. Catherine's icon of Christ as I softly and over and over again prayed the Jesus Prayer, "Lord Jesus Christ, Son of the Living God, have mercy on me, a sinner," letting the Spirit guide me into a deep state of prayer.

Gazing at the icon, I would then ask questions. This is a classic way of praying with an icon. I would ask, "Dear Jesus, what would you say to me tonight?" and "What would you say to my readers?" I would get a profound spiritual sense of what that might be—sometimes in words, other times in feelings—and then write it out. I do not consider this an extraordinary happening but a normal process of seeking intimacy with God.

The messages in this book are divided into four sections: Feel the Lord's Love, Learn about the Lord, Take Comfort in the Lord, and Feel Amazement in the Lord's Presence. At the end of each section are reflection questions that you may choose to journal about or simply ponder in the quiet of your heart. They are designed to help you to enter more profoundly into relationship with Jesus and others.

I invite you to encounter Jesus through these messages, Scripture passages, and prayers, to know how much he cares for you and wants to be intimately connected to you. Perhaps these messages will inspire you to approach Jesus in this way through your own imaginative and contemplative prayer, to open your heart and mind to Jesus, and to allow him to speak the words and messages he wants most for you to hear.

You might want to read one a day as a daily devotional, or simply read them through. You may want to keep this book handy and read messages that help you in times of need. You might want to use some combination of the ways we have just mentioned.

Feel *the* Lord's Love

I Cannot Contain My Love for You

My child, I am calling you to a journey, a journey into the core of my love, a love that so spills out from me I cannot contain it, a love so intimate it heals. Draw near me, for I am as close to you as you are to yourself.

As you are sitting there, reading this message, know that I embrace you, I touch you, and I kiss your heart. I invite you into an intimate friendship. Follow me as I lead you throughout these messages, and your life will sparkle with my brightness. I delight in you, even though you see yourself as wounded and limited.

My love comes from the heart of all eternity. My love is like an ocean, endless in its depths. My love is wonder, joy, singing, and dancing. My vestments are creation, which is beautiful beyond measure.

My love is touchable in those who are so easy to reject. Connect with the outcast and the vulnerable, and you connect with me.

Touch my body under the appearance of wine and bread, for I am of the earth, touchable, as real as your own body, as touchable as the bodies of your family and those for whom you care.

SCRIPTURE
Though the mountains fall away and the hills be shaken, my love shall never fall away from you nor my covenant of peace be shaken, says the Lord, who has mercy on you.
✝ Isaiah 54:10

PRAYER
Lord, help me to feel your love, to know that you are always with me. Help me to open my heart to you in intimate friendship and to, in turn, share your love with others. Amen.

My Love Always Pours Out for You

My child, my love is pouring out of me now for you. I will slow us down as we go on daily in this journey, to talk over the specifics of your life. But for now, I cannot contain myself. I am living and breathing, and my desire is to live and breathe with you every day. Let us draw close, ever closer, as I ask you questions about your life. What is it that is giving you happiness in your life right now? What brings joy? Think about that a moment. My love is like that love but greater. Know that as you walk with me in these messages, I can warm your heart into happiness and love you into joy, for I have abundant joy.

Stop a moment and think of times you have experienced love. Perhaps you are remembering a time when you were little and your parents or grandparents doted on you. Perhaps your parents and relatives did not dote on you but met you with hardness and coldness. I was there with you during that time. In moments of belief, when you have had that tug at your heart that something more than what you could see in front of you cherished you, that was me reaching out to you.

You have touched me in the kiss of husband and wife. You have touched me rocking your newborn infant. You have touched me in teaching your children the good in life, in playing with them, reading to them, ruffling the hair on their heads. These are tastes of my love.

SCRIPTURE
Taste and see that the Lord is good;
blessed is the stalwart one who takes refuge in him.
☩ PSALM 34:9

PRAYER
Dear Jesus, I know that you are near to me. Help me to sense your presence, to feel your love in the relationships I have with those closest to me. Help them to sense your love when I care for them. Amen.

The Infinity of My Caring

My child, the most important thing I want you to know is my love for you. This is the stupendous good news that underlies the universe. All stars, all galaxies, all light, a beautiful waterfall, the majesty of nearby mountains, a mother caressing the cheek of her infant with her hand—all are my creation, my apparel, my robe. The whole universe, every particle of creation, comprises my vestments. If you look hard enough, prayerfully enough, at creation around you, you can grasp some of the infinity of my caring.

Through these messages, I am calling you to a richer love, a deep-seated knowledge. My love for you is vast, vaster than the universe. My love for you is bigger than the greatest oceans. Even the infinity of space cannot describe the lengths and depths of my love for you. I love you in small ways also, through the little things in your daily life. I love you tenderly. I am nearer to you than your heartbeat and your breath.

My child, I can help you face your closely held secrets, your most acute inner ache. I was broken for you; let my brokenness mend yours. There is no fault so entrenched, no sin so gruesome, that I cannot wash it clean with the medicine of my mercy. I can come to you and cradle you when you need to weep. Come to me. Let me liberate your life, cast aside all your darkness, and infuse you with the same dance of joy that I dance. Trust me with your secrets. I will be as tender with you as a parent gently wiping away the tears from an infant's cheek.

SCRIPTURE

Come to me, all you who labor and are burdened, and I will give you rest. Take my yoke upon you and learn from me, for I am meek and humble of heart; and you will find rest for yourselves. For my yoke is easy, and my burden light.
✝ MATTHEW 11:28–30

PRAYER

Dear Lord, your love is vast, yet I can feel you stir within me. While your love is far away, other, it becomes amazingly near in your incarnation. Your love can be everyday love found in the daily stuff of living yet rooted in eternity itself. Help me to pour out my emotions and struggles to you each day. I know you will ease me and love me and thoroughly listen. Amen.

Pour Out Your Feelings to Me

MY CHILD, MY LOVE FOR YOU ENDURES FOREVER. The psalmist in Psalm 118 says many times: "For his steadfast love for you will endure forever." The psalmist was making it clear that I love you for all eternity. I love you in your weakness. I love you in your confusion. I love you in your disappointment. I love you in your joy and in your love. My love never ceases for you. It is like a huge reservoir of water behind a dam that goes on forever and ever. It goes on for eternity. That reservoir is the reservoir of my love, and I let you experience this as it flows through the dam a little bit at a time. My steadfast love endures amid your tragedies. My steadfast love endures when you fail. My steadfast love endures when you fall and turn again to me. I embrace you as the father embraced the wayward son in the gospel.

It is easy for you to build up and place on your shoulders all the things that go wrong, all your seeming failures and weaknesses. My love is yours forever. I take the burden from your shoulders and place them on to mine. In my coming to earth, I brought my love, and I call you to be spreaders of that same love. On my cross and in my taking on your humanity, I reconciled you despite your failings. Imitate me. Participate in the work of reconciliation among all those you see each week. Work on letting go of grudges. Work on letting go of an anger that at its heart wants to destroy and diminish. Come to me with those emotions. Pour out your feelings to me—that is the safe way to handle them—and I will replace them with a reconciling heart. I came into the world to establish my kingdom of love, joy, peace, and reconciliation, a world of compassion, a world enchanted by my newness. I have put my love on you and will never take it away. Without my coming, without this spreading of my love, the Bible is a mere prayer book of my stories and principles. This love is what makes the Bible pertinent. It is the story of my steadfast ability to love you and take care of you no matter what.

SCRIPTURE

In this way the love of God was revealed to us: God sent his only Son into the world so that we might have life through him. In this is love: not that we have loved God, but that he loved us and sent his Son as expiation for our sins.

✝ 1 John 4:9–10

PRAYER

Dear Lord, there are times in my life I carry a load on my shoulders, a load of responsibilities, a load of worry. At times, the load gets too large. It stoops me over. Remind me at such times that I do not have to bear it by myself. Remind me I can lay it at your feet. You care so much for me you even take the pile of my worry from me. Amen.

I Can Swoop You Up in My Embrace

MY CHILD, PERHAPS YOU ARE DISCOURAGED. Perhaps hurt grips your heart. Maybe the one you so loved is no longer there to love you back. Perhaps your life appears to have no purpose. You may find that anxiety and nervousness frequently tighten your chest or that you find little hope. Don't be afraid. I can impart my love for you in the middle of trying times.

In a moment, I can swoop you up into my embrace and you can taste the sweetness of my love, savoring the fullness of my beauty. My embrace is eternity's secret balm and medicine and can be a curative for all anxiety and discontent. You will travel to me and with me. As you read these messages, let the sea billows of my everlasting nurture sweep over you. You will swim in wonder. For the reality is that you have messages within you too: messages from the Spirit stirring within you, messages from Scripture planted in the inner chambers of your heart. In those messages I say, "Come to me. Let down your load and let eternity erupt from within you. You are very dear to me and I can bind you tenderly to me with cords of love."

As you read the messages in this book, your own messages can be released, for I am always talking to you. Cling to me as the child clings to the parent and I will make all things brand-new and sparkling for you. Through these messages, I am calling you to nothing less than a fathomless love, a deep-seated knowledge.

SCRIPTURE

For I am convinced that neither death, nor life, nor angels, nor principalities, nor present things, nor future things, nor powers, nor height, nor depth, nor any other creature will be able to separate us from the love of God in Christ Jesus our Lord. ✝ ROMANS 8:38–39

PRAYER

Lord, your love is unfathomable, yet you can whisper it in my soul. When life becomes too much for me, you can encircle me with your curing touch. Help me to say yes to you each day, so you can transfigure me with your love. Amen.

I Am Tenderhearted with Your Struggles

MY CHILD, MY LOVE FOR YOU IS NOT ONLY EVERLASTING; IT IS PATIENT. So often, selfishness can take hold in a myriad of ways. Instead of saying "we," you say "me." How easy it is to relate everything with reference to yourself, to "what pleases me." When relationships are measured only by whether the other person meets your needs, lashing out at others can easily become the norm. Self-absorption can create disruption all around you and drain the joy from life. Terrible misunderstandings ensue. Envision for a moment a four-year-old boy whose mother comes out of a grocery store on a blistering day with bulging sacks of groceries. He demands she go back in and get him a candy bar. Firmly but gently, she says no, and they proceed to the car where she sweeps him up in a hug and assures that all is well but tells him that love often means being patient and thinking about how your demands affect others. Think of the father in the parable who embraced and celebrated his son's return from the far country. Please know, dear children, that this is how patient I am with you.

I am tenderhearted with your struggles, patient with your

self-seeking. No matter what types of selfishness and self-seeking you get tied up in in life, no matter the harm that you may do to yourself and those you hurt by your selfishness, know that I am waiting, eyes glistening, ready to forgive. I am waiting like the mother at the grocery store and the devoted father of the parable. Simply turn to me. I am waiting to enfold you with my bottomless mercy and my life-saving tenderness.

SCRIPTURE
While he was still a long way off, his father caught sight of him, and was filled with compassion. He ran to his son, embraced him, and kissed him. His son said to him, "Father, I have sinned against heaven and against you; I no longer deserve to be called your son." But his father ordered his servants, "Quickly bring the finest robe and put it on him; put a ring on his finger and sandals on his feet, because this son of mine was dead, and has come to life again; he was lost, and has been found." ✟ LUKE 15:20–24

PRAYER
Dear Lord, you know me so well. Many times, I become so self-absorbed, so selfish, that I hurt others and myself. I need your forgiveness, your mercy, which comes in the bosom of my heart and in hearing the priest say: "I absolve you." Give me the courage to come to you when I fail. May the quality of your love lead me outside myself so that I may love others as you love them. Amen.

I Am Always with You

My child, my love for you is in the breaking of the bread and the drinking of the wine as you eat and drink my Body and my Blood. When you are broken, like the Eucharist is broken, know that I can be with you. Just as the host is broken and yet still whole, so can I heal your brokenness with my brokenness. When you anguish and are in deep despair, if you come to me, I will lift you up. When there seems no pathway ahead, I will make a pathway for you. My love for you is like the Father's love: strong, firm, and gentle with the special strong gentleness that *fathers can feel*. Have you ever felt the burdens of the world weigh so heavily upon you and then finally a friend listens and you're able to inwardly break out in song because you know that someone is with you? I will always listen to you, be present with you, and love you.

My caring is found in the depths of your being, in your heartbeat, in your breath. I am nearer to you than your heartbeat and your breath. I am with you when you are caught up in fear, resentment, and isolation. I am there to give you a strong hand to pull you up. When you are facing behaviors and things in your life you cannot change by yourself, you can call to me. I am the higher power who will give you aid when no aid seems possible. I come to you through my word spoken through the prophets, all Scripture, the Eucharist, and finally in my love made touchable in my incarnation.

SCRIPTURE

Then he took the bread, said the blessing, broke it, and gave it to them, saying, "This is my body, which will be given for you; do this in memory of me." And likewise the cup after they had eaten, saying, "This cup is the new covenant in my blood, which will be shed for you."
✝ Luke 22:19–20

PRAYER

Jesus, thank you for the gift of the Eucharist. When I receive you under the appearance of bread or wine, help me to open my heart to be truly united with you. Help me to always believe that you are truly present with me, always loving me and listening to my prayers. Please heal the brokenness in my life. Amen.

I Love You with an Everlasting Love

My child, my love for you is as real as your breathing and heartbeat. My love is down-to-earth, approachable. You see, I know what it is to live your life. I was as totally and fully human as you. I ate, drank, and slept as you do. I felt joy and sorrow as you have felt joy and sorrow. I grew hungry, tired, and anxious.

I felt the normal human emotions. I was hurt when people rejected me, just as you may have been rejected. I longed for love as you do. I laughed, and I wept. My heart widened in the presence of friends who loved me, and I was deeply hurt when friends deserted me. Therefore, I know your burdens; I suffer in your losses. I know what it is you need. I love you simply because you are. Broken, sinful, or alone—you are mine and you belong to me. I feel your joys, laugh in your laughter, and lament with you in the bitter times. I weep with you in your tears.

My love is vast. My love is pure. My message to you is the same message spoken in Jeremiah: "I have loved you with an everlasting love." My love is an ocean of caring that can embrace you, brighten your life, and mend your soul. My love meets your needs if you only accept it. My love can fill you with self-worth. My love can fill you with well-being. My love will make you feel lovable. My love for you burns like fire. Fire warms. Fire gives light. I want to surround you in a living flame of love that originates from the very heart of eternity.

So, my friend, talk to me. Unburden yourself with me. If you are ruffled by life, I can soothe you. If you are overcome with sin, I can forgive you. If you need to change, I can help you change. Keep your eyes fixed on me. You are not alone. Your void need not consume you.

SCRIPTURE
With age-old love I have loved you; so I have kept my mercy toward you. ✛ Jeremiah 31:3

PRAYER
Dear Lord, it can be scary to think that you know all of me, even the parts I want so much to hide. Please help me to feel your love even when I don't feel lovable. Amen.

Allow the Living Flame of My Love to Burn in You

My child, Moses saw the burning bush in the wilderness. The flame flared, but it did not consume the bush. The fire's source was eternal; it burns for ages unto ages. The burning flame does not destroy the bush. The whole universe is a burning bush. The fire of my love spreads through all things. The symbol of the burning bush is an eternal symbol of my love for you and creation throughout the universe. This is also a sign of pure compassion, cleansing, and a love that does not consume you but engages you totally. The bush symbolizes an eternal compassion that cleanses all things and transforms and transfigures that which it enflames. It is, as St. John of the Cross intimates, a "living flame of love." Turn your heart to me and you can be transfigured by the living flame of my love. My love is a flame you can spread to everyone you meet if you will just open your heart to it. I am calling on you to say yes to my love, yes to the flame in the bosom of your soul, yes to the flame of your actions. Picture the flame in your prayer; picture the flame in your reaching out and loving others by spreading the fire. The bush reveals who I am to you. The burning flame reveals who I am to you: the one who is the source of fiery love for all eternity.

What I am speaking to you now, my child, in these messages is not a new revelation, but things I have said to humans from the beginning through revelation of God to the Hebrew people and most of all in the new covenant I made with my body and blood and life in my incarnation. What you hear will be consistent with what has always been said in nature, in the bosom of your soul, in Scripture, and in the Church. Allow me to immerse you in the flame of love with which I immerse the universe. Allow my presence to so burn in you that you love the ones I love and love the things I love, and love in me and with me the whole creation and your fellow humans, your brothers and sisters in Christ.

SCRIPTURE

There the angel of the Lord appeared to him as fire flaming out of a bush. When he looked, although the bush was on fire, it was not being consumed.

✝ Exodus 3:2

PRAYER

Dear Lord, fill me with the living flame of your love. Allow it to burn with me, to transform and transfigure me so that I may in turn carry the light of your love to others. Amen.

I Love Your True Self

MY CHILD, YOU TRULY DO NOT KNOW YOURSELF. You do not fully know what I am to you. And you do not know the potential my love brings. I look on you and see you and your mistakes and your selfishness. I see your deep self, which abides under that. That is the self I wish to reach out to. My love can forgive. My love can cleanse. My love can make you fresh. For my love for you is for your deep and true self. It is so easy to wear masks, to conceal your true self from other people. You even try to conceal yourself from me, but I see under those masks. I look past those masks into your heart, into the child within, into your true self. Others do not fully understand you. You do not fully understand yourself, but I am the one who understands you and cherishes you and is glad that you are my child. No matter what you might have done in the past, I can lift you up and get you up straight and walking. I can cut you from the chains that you may have been chained to and set you free to love others in the ways you have been loved.

Loving others can seem difficult at times. If you are cold, warm yourself by the heater. If you are in the dark, turn on the light switch and there will be light. If you find it hard to love others, if selfishness obstructs your heart, come taste my love, and selfishness will begin to dissolve. Turn away from yourself and gaze upon me. My love kindled in your heart is the best means of kindling your love toward others.

SCRIPTURE

Lord, you have probed me, you know me: you know when I sit and when I stand; you understand my thoughts from afar. You sift through my travels and my rest; with all my ways you are familiar. Where can I go from your spirit? From your presence, where can I flee?

✝ PSALMS 139:1–3, 7

PRAYER

My Lord, all too often I hide who I am from others. I fear that if I show who I truly am, they will reject me. I even try to hide from you, but you are always with me. You know everything about me and still love me. Help me to trust in that love and to open myself to you. Help me to share all that I am with you. Amen.

Reflection Questions

Think back over your life. When have you most felt the love of God? What did it feel like to bask in that love?

Who was/is the person who has loved you the most? How did/does that person show their love? What have you learned from that person about how to show love to others? How can you show God's love to others, especially those who are difficult to love?

Do you ever feel that there are parts of you that are unworthy of love? Are there parts of you that you try to hide from others? Are there parts of you that you try to hide from God? What would it feel like to reveal all of who you are to God? Can you trust in God's love?

Jesus is always present in the Eucharist. Have you ever been to adoration? If not, is there a way you could make time in your schedule to spend some quiet time with the Lord in front of a tabernacle or monstrance? What does it feel like to simply rest in the Lord's presence?

Learn about *the* Lord

Scripture Is a Speedway into Your Heart

My child, all the Scripture leads to me. I have given it to you, not simply to understand, though understanding is important, but to wash over and through you. In Scripture, you see the tenderness with which I loved Israel, my disciples, and everyone. Its words can rearrange your day. Reading Scripture daily is genuinely a light to your path and a lamp to your feet. More than mere words, it is a speedway that I can travel into your heart. The rhythms of Scripture are the heartbeat of my love for you.

Look at Scripture not just with your head but with your entire being, and it will flow through you. When you read Scripture, slow down. If possible, read it out loud, cherishing each word.

Scripture also challenges you to enfold the sojourner, the homeless, the poor, the widow, the lonely, those easily despised; enfold them in your care in the same way I enfold you.

SCRIPTURE

How sweet to my tongue is your promise,
  sweeter than honey to my mouth!
Through your precepts I gain understanding;
  therefore I hate all false ways.
Your word is a lamp for my feet,
  a light for my path.
✝ PSALMS 119:103–105

PRAYER

Dear Lord, in the rhythms of Scripture, I find the rhythms of your very own heartbeat. When I read it, you nurture my soul, and I can feel the waves of your love flow throughout me. Remind me daily of the treasure that is the Bible. Teach me to savor its words slowly as a lover savors the love of his beloved. Amen.

I Call You to Work Miracles

My child, I showed the might of my love in healings and miracles. Through prayer, you can also work miracles. You can become a curer of souls, a mender of persons. All your prayer can become a holy burning in your heart, a fire that warms and sustains you in the center of your being. Your personality can be so imbued with me that you become a holy, life-giving image of me to the people you meet.

Take time in quiet and in praise to open wide to my presence. Reaching out to me can be an enormous pleasure, an enormous joy that transforms you into a joy-bringer to all you meet. Prayer is a time when you will be reconstructed, when you bear the innermost workings of your soul to me: the past pain, the past joys, the past accomplishments, your deep search for meaning, your shame, your good and wonderful times. Prayer allows you to feel pain you may have pretended was not there, hurt that you ignored. It allows you to invite my love in, to bring the salve of a great and a wonderful medicine.

The result is not so much that you proclaim the gospel.

Rather, you become the gospel, becoming through me a miracle worker and a healer.

SCRIPTURE
"Amen, I say to you, if you have faith the size of a mustard seed, you will say to this mountain, 'Move from here to there,' and it will move. Nothing will be impossible for you.'"
✝ MATTHEW 17:20

PRAYER
Dear Lord, in your earthly life you performed many miracles, healing bodies and souls. I know that you are also calling me to be a mender of what is torn, a worker of miracles of the heart. Daily soak me in your love so that I may spread the aroma of that love to all I meet. Give me deep sensitivity to the needs of others, just as you show deep sensitivity to me. Help my breathing, my walking, and my doing become emblems of miracle to others. Amen.

Drink of My Living Water

MY CHILD, DURING MY LIFE HERE ON EARTH, I WAS OFTEN EXHAUSTED AND OVERWORKED. As a human being, I often endured all the fatigue and weariness you endure. When I came to Jacob's well and asked the woman there for a drink, I sat down because I was exhausted and drained. When I asked the woman for a drink, it was not just the way to open a conversation. I was actually thirsty. I fully participated in all the limits, weaknesses, and fatigue that all humans experience.

Long before Calvary, I lived the stresses and the struggles, the joys and the fatigue of being human. I did this to show that it is not only through my death that you are redeemed but through the totality of my being human and facing human limitations, including needing a drink from a Samaritan woman, wanting to be near the coolness of the well. Weary and reclining on Jacob's well was a sign of my work, my mission carrying me to the edge of my capabilities. It is through my everydayness, sharing your limitations, that you are saved, not just through the cross. And I understand how hard it is for you. I participated in the humanity I redeem.

Therefore, I can be right there with you in your walk through life, the same walk I walked. I can hold you close as you go about your life, showing you that your struggles can be gateways to glory. When you are depleted and thirsty, I can offer you a drink from the living water. When things seem altogether too much for you, I can let you rest in my arms.

Just as I reach out to you, you can reach out to other weary souls, offering the solace that only those who have experienced my presence in the midst of human struggle can offer.

SCRIPTURE

Jesus answered and said to her, "Everyone who drinks this water will be thirsty again; but whoever drinks the water I shall give will never thirst; the water I shall give will become in him a spring of water welling up to eternal life."
✝ JOHN 4:13–14

PRAYER

Thank you, Lord, that you understand how weary and worn out I get. Teach me to turn to you for refreshment and a drink of living water when things seem to be "too much" for me. Amen.

I Call You to Love and Service

My child, I love you so much, I wish for you to share in my glory. I want you to live a life enchanted by the truly holy and sacred. I want your life to tingle with the brightness of eternity. In short, I want you to be drawn into the innermost chambers of my heart. Even in the midst of daily living, this is possible.

To really experience the infinity of my boundless love, I want you to begin to love and serve others the way I love and serve you. This at first may seem too daunting, lonely, and hard. You may be so keenly aware of your own limitations. There is no need to fret, for if you invite me to help you, take my hand, and let me help you tread along the pathway of becoming a loving servant who loves and serves others, I will begin to change you so much that you will deeply desire to pour out your love in service to others. Prayer can change you; so can sacraments and fellowship with other believers.

But the truth is that reaching out to others will all too often not be an easy pathway. All too often, my child, you want to live a spiritual life that is free of dust and heat, thirst and weariness. I've lived a human life through those things. You must serve others in the midst of such adversity. You must endure that adversity if you are to follow me, for it is in the midst of such things that you experience perfect joy. You have a mission, my children, to love others, to free them in the ways that I have freed you, to care about those who are most despised. That's what I did, and that's what you are called to do. And I will guide and lead you all the way. I will aide you in each act of kindness. You have a mission, but you also have a Sender, one who sends as a loving Father, who has spoken through me.

SCRIPTURE
"The righteous will answer him and say, 'Lord, when did we see you hungry and feed you, or thirsty and give you drink? When did we see you a stranger and welcome you, or naked and clothe you? When did we see you ill or in prison, and visit you?' And the king will say to them in reply, 'Amen, I say to you, whatever you did for one of these least brothers of mine, you did for me.'" ✛ **MATTHEW 25:39–40**

PRAYER
Dear Jesus, help me to follow you even in the midst of the adversity of life. Help me to love and serve you by loving and serving others. Help me to see you in everyone I meet. Amen.

Seek Me in Scripture

My child, even the infinity of space cannot describe the lengths and depths of my love for you. I love you in small ways too. I love you tenderly. As a mother nurses her child, so can my love nurture you. As a brother puts his hand on the shoulder of a sibling and says, "I know what it is like to live through what you are living through," I take your hand and pat you on your back. When you are hurting, I can be right there with you to warm your heart and body with the infinity of my caring.

Seek my love in Scripture. Let the very words of Scripture entrance you. Be pulled into the account of my mighty acts. In those accounts you will find people delivered from sin and self-destructive behavior. You will see the ebb and flow of my Spirit for my Spirit breathes in every word of Scripture. Go beyond the surface of the words and you will find me.

If you are to know my love, let Scripture be your companion day and night. Enter with your whole self into the words you read; for Scripture is my story, but it is also your story. You will discover yourself afresh and discover me afresh when you ponder the words, chewing them like a cow chews its cud.

SCRIPTURE

"One does not live by bread alone, but by every word that comes forth from the mouth of God."

✛ Matthew 4:4

PRAYER

Lord, help me to love your word in Scripture. Help me to get to know you more deeply and to trust in your mighty power and your love for me. Amen.

Immerse Yourself in the Glorious and the True

MY CHILD, I HAVE TWO MYSTERIES I CALL YOU INTO.

The first is this: that which is absolutely free costs everything. Anyone may touch my love without cost. But when you touch it, you become different. Love takes you into the crucible of change until you begin to pour out your heart and love in the manner I love. Open yourself to that scary, risky love.

The second mystery is this: that which is apart is tied together. Feel compassion move outward, radiating through unseen cords to countless others. The cords knit you all together with me and each other. Each of you is a universe of individuality, yet you are also united as one, embraced by one love. Each pain of the other was my pain, each joy my joy. Your pain and joy are my pain and joy.

You are not redeemed alone. You are not made whole alone. You are healed together. Yours is not a solitary questing but a questing with one another. As you pray for others, you are mended. As you touch the hearts of others, your heart is repaired. Only as you forget yourself in love of the other, only as you fall in love with my love, will you then discover yourself.

SCRIPTURE
As a body is one though it has many parts, and all the parts of the body, though many, are one body, so also Christ.... God has so constructed the body as to give greater honor to a part that is without it, so that there may be no division in the body, but that the parts may have the same concern for one another. If one part suffers, all the parts suffer with it; if one part is honored, all the parts share its joy.
✝ 1 Corinthians 12:12, 24–26

PRAYER
Jesus, help me to feel united to all your people. Help me to lose myself in loving you and others. Teach me that my yearning for you is not a lonely yearning but a longing I share with all of my brothers and sisters in the world and the whole of creation. Amen.

Draw Close to Me through Other People

MY CHILD, DRAWING CLOSE TO ME MEANS DRAWING CLOSE TO OTHER PEOPLE. Life is not a solo journey. My life was not a solo journey. My profound relationship with the Father, my relationship with Mary and Joseph, and my relationships with my followers strengthened me and also often challenged me. I had special relationships, people I loved deeply, such as Peter and the Beloved Disciple who rested on my bosom at my last meal. Mary, Martha, and Lazarus were close friends. Mary of Magdala's affirmation helped me carry on my mission.

You also were born in relationship. Even before you were born, you were relating to others. You were in relationship to your birth mother; then others came into your life. Some relationships are casual: the store clerk, the mail carrier, the bus driver. Other relationships are far more important; they touch your depths. Relationships with family, friends, teachers, spouse, and those in the Church can be deep and meaningful.

One way to look at relationships is to see each life as an individual thread. By itself one thread is not impressive, but when we weave the threads of many lives together, a beautiful textured cloth can emerge, giving great purpose to your life. Whenever you make time to build positive relationships, not only are your relationships enriched, but your vitality and health are improved. You move beyond merely existing to truly living. Relationships allow me to sculpt you into the fully alive human being I intended you to be from all eternity.

Loving others is part of your love relationship with me. As my servant Augustine put it: "The love with which we love God and love one another is the same love." Maturity involves meeting me in human relationships as well as in solitude. Prayer that moves us away from people can become escapism. Prayer and people belong together. Relationship is not a means to a goal; it is the goal.

Just as other people channel God's love to you, so you can be a channel of God's love to others. The fruit of prayer is not beautiful religious experiences while we pray—though if those do happen, they should be received with gratitude. The true fruit of prayer comes in the midst of your everyday life and relationships.

SCRIPTURE

"I give you a new commandment: love one another. As I have loved you, so you also should love one another. This is how all will know that you are my disciples, if you have love for one another." ✝ JOHN 13:34–35

PRAYER

Dear Lord, you call us to love one another. That is not always an easy task. Sometimes it seems like it is hardest to love those I spend the most time with. Help me to always see you in them and to share your love with them. Help me to treasure the close relationships in my life. Amen.

My Living Water Can Purify You

MY CHILD, I COME TO YOU THROUGH THE LITTLE THINGS OF YOUR DAILY LIFE. I come to you in the water you use each day. The water cleanses you, takes away the dirt, makes you fresh and clean. Water washes you. I refresh you and cleanse you through water. I revive your heart as I revive your body. I revive you through water. I am not only the giver of water; I am the one who gives you living water. With water, I can make a dry field blossom with grain or vegetables. I can make an arid field able to produce. With my living water, I can help you become fruitful and full of love for all things and all people. As water flows over your face when you wash yourself, think of the ways you at times stumble and how I wash those stumbles away.

Through my living water, I make your soul able to produce the fruit of the Spirit. In the morning, I give you regular water to wash your face, get you clean with, and wake you up. The water that wakes you up in the morning is a mere symbol. The living water I give you is as real as eternity. My living water wakes you up and makes you alive and aware of the world around you, a world that is full of my presence. I am the living water that washes your soul as surely as regular water washes your body.

My living water quenches your thirst for all eternity. So daily let me purify you with this living water, clearing away the smudges of self-absorption. Just as you bless yourself with holy water, so you can bless others with the peace of my presence.

SCRIPTURE

On the last and greatest day of the feast, Jesus stood up and exclaimed, "Let anyone who thirsts come to me and drink. Whoever believes in me, as scripture says, 'Rivers of living water will flow from within him.'" ✛ JOHN 7:37–38

PRAYER

Dear Lord, please give me your living water. Please cleanse my soul of its impurities so that I may better share the peace you offer me with others. Amen.

In Serving Others, You Serve Me

My child, I showed at my Last Supper how water could cleanse feet. It is a symbolic cleansing of the whole of the person, wiping away the grime, wiping away the little stones. At that supper, Peter had protested and said, "Lord, are you going to wash my feet?" I told him, "Unless I wash you, you will have no inheritance with me." My desire for you, my dear child, is that you have a part of me, so that daily, wherever you are, you let me wash your feet. I can reach down into your anxiety, into your self-blaming, your fear, your inadequacy with the quality of my understanding and care.

My child, I wash your feet with my towel. Your impurities disappear as my water flows over them. Water is a constant reminder of the reality of baptism. "No one can enter the kingdom of God without being born of water and Spirit." I have come to you in the waters of baptism. There are other waters that can cleanse you and make you fresh. The waters of repentance, turning to me, turning away from that which stifles our relationship, to receive my full embrace. This water is the water of your tears. When hurts from the past take root in you and you see my hands wash your feet gently, know how much I love you, how much I suffered for you. When you see that, be open to tears that carry you into the eternity of my love. And with those tears, you might want to wash and anoint my feet just as the woman anointed me with tears and perfume.

With all the tenderness that is in you, you can wash my feet. You can wash my feet in caring for the poorest of the poor, the homeless and the sick, the rejected, those who face a life of discrimination, people of different races. The water in which you are baptized, with which you wash, also means a washing of blood. When they stuck a spear in my side, I bled both water and blood. The water of Calvary and the baptismal water of the Jordan mingled. That is the purification of your spirit.

SCRIPTURE

Now there was a sinful woman in the city who learned that he was at table in the house of the Pharisee. Bringing an alabaster flask of ointment, she stood behind him at his feet weeping and began to bathe his feet with her tears. Then she wiped them with her hair, kissed them, and anointed them with ointment. ✢ Luke 7:37–38

PRAYER

Lord, help me tenderly to touch and wash your feet as the woman did, and allow me to have this same attitude toward those who suffer. Help me to serve and to care for all those who suffer. Help me to know that when I serve and care for them, I serve and care for you. Amen.

I Can Give You an Abundant Life

MY CHILD, I AM AN ENORMOUS AND TREMENDOUS LOVER. My love is the ground of the cosmos, all creation, and your very existence. I love you, body and soul, down to the very cells of your fingernails. I want you to say yes to that love through this grace, love me in return, and love all that I love. My enormous love became touchable, real, down-to-earth, everyday love in my incarnation; it remains physical and tangible in the Eucharist.

Through these messages I am helping you embrace spirituality, loving me and all that I love. Spirituality is about what matters most to you. What mattered most to me was my relationship to the Father and bringing in the kingdom of God. Through encountering me in Scripture, the sacraments, and the Church, you may discover that what matters most to you in the core of your being may not be what you may have thought it to be. It may well be your hunger for God and the kingdom of God. As you talk to me in prayer, as you rest on my bosom in contemplation as did the Beloved Disciple, you will discover that my love and all that I love are what are truly central. This does not happen in an instance; it is a process. As this unfolds you will find a big adventure that will excite you in the core of your being and open new lands and horizons in life. It is about life as I put it: "I came that you might have life and have it more abundantly" (John 10:10).

You have spirituality within you by being a child of God. Often what is needed is just to dive in. Spirituality is not so much about climbing a ladder toward perfection or running an obstacle course successfully as it is about grace—my love reaching down and elevating you. It is not about being a spiritual competitor but about holding out a cup for me to fill.

SCRIPTURE
"I am the gate. Whoever enters through me will be saved, and will come in and go out and find pasture. A thief comes only to steal and slaughter and destroy; I came so that they might have life and have it more abundantly."
✟ JOHN 10:9–10

PRAYER
Dear Jesus, sometimes I get bogged down in the concerns of this world. It is all too easy to lose sight of what really matters. Help me to keep my eyes and my heart focused on you. Help me to realize that only you can infuse my life with meaning and give me the abundant life that you have promised to those who follow you. Amen.

Let Me Invade the Totality of Your Life

My child, spirituality, letting your heart and life be filled with me, involves far more than your religious side. It involves more than your soul. It involves the whole of you: your work, your school life, your family. There is not some special section in your hearts marked as "spiritual." Real encounters with me concern not only what you believe but, more important, how you see your world and yourself. Falling in love with me and all that I love concerns your hurts, your gifts, your creativity, and your relationships with others, especially the marginalized and the outcast.

It is all about seeing the world with fresh eyes, so fresh that it is like seeing it for the first time. It means looking for the hidden beauty and looking with my eyes, which means to look with love.

In prayer, you take the whole of your lives and let me soak it with the wonder of my caring. Spirituality that is pure navel gazing is a misshapen spirituality. Spirituality involves others, not just yourself. You need to go out and share that love with a world hungry for me.

Draw near to me each day. Take time to tell me the things that are important to you. Share your emotions with me, your gladness, your joy, but also your raw emotions, such as anger, shame, and embarrassment. In short, feel free to cry with me, to laugh with me.

When you do that, I can knit our hearts together. Spirituality involves talking with me as a friend, searching for me in the Scriptures, attuning your hearts as you touch my body and blood. It involves far more than personal prayer; it involves worshiping with others. It involves allowing me to invade the totality of your life.

SCRIPTURE
"You are my friends if you do what I command you. I no longer call you slaves, because a slave does not know what his master is doing. I have called you friends, because I have told you everything I have heard from my Father. It was not you who chose me, but I who chose you and appointed you to go and bear fruit that will remain, so that whatever you ask the Father in my name he may give you."
✝ JOHN 15:14–16

PRAYER
Dear Jesus, I want to be counted among your friends. I want to share my whole life with you. I want to share my joys and sorrows with you. I want to love you and follow you. Please take all that I am and infuse it with your light and your love. Amen.

I Want You to Reach Out to Others with Kindness

My child, throughout these messages, the thing I emphasize most is my love for you. Allowing me to love you carries you through a crucible of change. You more and more become someone who loves and is kind. More than my miracles, healings, and exorcisms, what drew people near to me was my kindness and compassion. I cared; I really cared. Few things carry the ability to change our world as simply being kind. Kindness shows love in action. The world hears the gospel when it sees it. I gave concrete examples of this type of kindness, and I call all my children to acts of kindness. Kindness is giving a cup of cold water, offering aid to someone who was beaten and left to suffer in a ditch, visiting prisoners, feeding the hungry, clothing those without clothes, and visiting the ill and the prisoner. Kindness was noticing enough, caring enough to feed five thousand people. My life was filled to the brim with acts of kindness.

Acts of kindness mean far more in my eyes than being an athletic star, an honor student, or a financial success. I demonstrated my kindness by healing the sick and showing compassion to the sinner. In a mighty act of kindness, while suffering on the cross, I showed generosity to the thief suffering beside me and welcomed him into my kingdom.

Often when someone first experiences my love, he or she tends to view the spiritual life as a roadway to personal fulfillment and a happier family life. While prayer does lead to personal fulfillment, true prayer eventually draws you beyond the purely personal. You begin to see that your individual healing is tied in with the healing of the whole world. Only as you open to the cry of the poor, to their pain, can the healing process begin within you.

Emptying yourself in service for the sake of others is at the heart of what it means to be a believer. Redemption involves the whole created universe.

Reaching out to others with kindness and compassion helps you become a servant who loves, serves, and accepts those who most need.

SCRIPTURE
"Then the king will say to those on his right, 'Come, you who are blessed by my Father. Inherit the kingdom prepared for you from the foundation of the world. For I was hungry and you gave me food, I was thirsty and you gave me drink, a stranger and you welcomed me, naked and you clothed me, ill and you cared for me, in prison and you visited me.'"
✢ MATTHEW 25:34–36

PRAYER

Dear Jesus, you call me to live out my faith by loving others. Help me to see you in all who are suffering. Help me to reach out to all who are in need, wherever and whenever I meet them. Help me to always respond with love and kindness. Let me be a sign of your love in the world. Amen.

Reflection Questions

We learn about the Lord through Scripture and prayer. Do you spend time each day reading some Scripture and conversing with the Lord in prayer? If not, is there a way you can incorporate this into your life, even if it is only for a few minutes a day? If you already do this, what can you do to make that Scripture reflection and prayer more meaningful in your life? What questions and problems do you want to bring to the Lord? How can you quiet your heart to better hear the message that Jesus wants you to hear?

Sometimes we are able to get to know the Lord through other people. Who do you know who radiates the Lord's love? What do they show you about how the Lord wants us to live?

What does it mean to you to become a living gospel? What message do you think that your life gives to other people? Do you think people can tell you are Christian by the way you live? If not, what needs to change? What is one concrete step you can take to better live the Lord's message?

Jesus said that he came to give us an abundant life. What does it mean to you to have an abundant life? What would that look like? Have you ever had a foretaste of eternal life in this world? When?

Take Comfort *in the* Lord

Taste the Deep Quiet of My Heart

MY CHILD, SLEEP OFTEN CAN RESTORE YOU. After a busy day and hectic evening, you fall asleep on a comfortable mattress, and a few hours later you are up and ready to go, feeling better, restored, rested. In the Scriptures, I say, "Come to me, all you who are tired and heavy-laden, and I will give you rest" (Mt 11:28). These messages that I give to you each day are so that you may rest, rest from your burdens, rest from the distresses of everyday living, and taste the deep quiet of my heart, which is like a still pond with unfathomable depths.

I invite you on a journey of rest and tranquility. So many things may jangle within you: fears from the past, distressed relationships that you may not have dealt with. Apprehension of the future, concern about what is over the next horizon, and worry for tomorrow may at times consume you. My touch can lighten your load and help you develop that rich quiet of the soul that will fill you up forever. My touch refreshes as it remakes.

I came down for you and live for you. I died on the cross for you. I sent my spirit upon you. I am as intimate to you as your own heartbeat and will always be with you. My love for you is boundless, without measure. And day by day as you go on your journey, I can give you a taste of it. My love is like floating on a rubber raft on the quiet lake of my peace; the stresses of your heart flow away, and anxiety seeps from your body and soul.

SCRIPTURE
Have no anxiety at all, but in everything, by prayer and petition, with thanksgiving, make your requests known to God. Then the peace of God that surpasses all understanding will guard your hearts and minds in Christ Jesus.
✢ PHILIPPIANS 4:6–7

PRAYER
Jesus, help me see more clearly the contours of my soul and the patterns of my thoughts. Help me touch this moment, this present, and give it to you so that you may flood me with your love and show me the seeds of eternity hidden in the ordinary things. Amen.

I Can Lighten Your Load

MY CHILD, AS YOU TOUCH BASE WITH ME EACH DAY, I can lighten your load and ease your fears.

When you were little, the world probably overwhelmed you with strange new noises, sights, and experiences. If you were gifted with a caring home, those around you reached out to you: your mother, your father, your whole family, and your friends. They reassured you as they wiped your tears away.

You need that same security as an adult—the comfort of someone feeling your feelings, hugging you with a touch that brings peace and calms the worst tumult.

Perhaps your home was not loving and supportive. Be assured I walked with you then.

Today when you find your world crushes in on you and you feel a load of sadness, I can cradle you with an inward embrace, brightening you as you travel through your day.

When there has been terrible loss, terrible misunderstanding, it can be like the despair my earliest disciples felt after my death and burial. And then, on the third day, there was a mighty happening, a return. My resurrection imparts the comfort of all comforts. I restore that which was lost. The wonder of the angels at my tomb and the wonder of my appearances can heal you after a lifetime of despair. My resurrection is a bursting light that can come unexpectedly to you in the inward parts of your soul. Just as I appeared to Mary Magdalene, to Peter, to the disciples, so I can appear to you. Perhaps my appearance to you is not the same as that with which I met my disciples, but in touching me, you touch the incredible newness of the kingdom, of a world whose despair and hurt I overcame, and your life too can be graced with the tenderness Thomas felt as he touched my risen side.

SCRIPTURE
"Peace I leave with you; my peace I give to you. Not as the world gives do I give it to you. Do not let your hearts be troubled or afraid." ✛ JOHN 14:27

PRAYER
Jesus, gently lead me into your ease so that I can extend your peace to all I meet and become for others a sign of your peace. Surround me with your great peacefulness, calm my heart, and make me ready to meet you in my living and in my prayer. Amen.

My Compassion Is Far Greater Than the Aches Within

My child, I come to you in your need. I comfort you in your distress. I lift you up when all seems hopeless. I cradle you with a compassion far greater than the aches within. However, while I am glad that you love me because of these things that I do for you, there is a deeper love I call you to.

The people around you can also help you: the carpool that gets you to work, or the help you receive from your coworkers at your job, for example. You can come to love people because of what they do for you. I am calling you to realize you need to love people *for who they are*. You really begin to love when you can see more than how relationships help you, when you can see a person for who they really are, for their uniqueness and personality, their kindheartedness, even their anger and distress. When you know a person, you are entered into a vastly richer way of love.

So it is with me. I do things for you. I take your hand amid the worst trouble you could go through, but I yearn for more than this. I yearn for you to fall in love with me. I yearn for you to love me for myself. So, every day as I give so much help to you, know that I long to give you much more. I long to set your heart afire with an infinite beauty.

SCRIPTURE
"You shall love the Lord, your God, with all your heart, with all your souls, and with all your mind. This is the greatest and the first commandment. The second is like it: You shall love your neighbor as yourself." ✝ **Matthew 22:37–39**

PRAYER
Jesus, guide my prayer as I face my buried fears. I turn fear over to the comfort and love that surrounds my every breath, the mystery that follows my every step. This mystery abides with me in times of desolation, accompanies me when I'm in despair, revives me in my seasons of consolation, and banishes the dark and the shadows. Amen.

Never Forget That I Am in the Boat with You

MY CHILD, MANY STORMS MAY COME YOUR WAY, not only physical storms like a hurricane, but storms of the emotions, storms of expectations. Someone who is close to you begins to turn hostile toward you and stays that way for a while, and you struggle with how to heal, how to draw close, and how to contain the anger that is rising up in you because of this. Storms may happen when you lose a job, lose a spouse, or stay up at night worrying if your child will turn out okay after all.

My disciples worried on the boat with me when a terrible storm came up, and I calmed the storm. So it is with you. You may have those storms, but never forget that I am in the boat with you. I can calm the storm of your heart. It may not be just in the way you would like, but I can calm you. I can calm the storm clouds and even the waves in your heart. No matter what kind of things you have been worrying about—stress at work, problems in marriage, depression, or anxiety—when those storms come up, remember that I am the great calmer of storms. As surely as I calmed the boat in the storm for my disciples, I can calm your boat. I can calm the eruptions in your own life.

Do not think your losses, your setbacks, your emotional storms only leave you scarred. They often lead to great benefit because, after you have experienced a pain, a loss, the poor opinion of others, or things just not working out, you can come through those experiences with a greater compassion for others; it is easier to love others who go through storms, who go through pains, because you have too. In fact, the rocks of distress in your gunnysack can be turned to jewels when you allow them to develop within you a lasting heart of compassion.

SCRIPTURE
They set sail, and while they were sailing he fell asleep. A squall blew over the lake, and they were taking in water and were in danger. They came and woke him saying, "Master, master, we are perishing!" He awakened, rebuked the wind and the waves, and they subsided and there was a calm. ✝ Luke 8:22–24

PRAYER
Jesus, I hand over my tension, my fears, my anxiety. Soften my heart with your nearness. Shine your light along the roads I take. And always, in every place, may I soothe, comfort, and cherish others in the way that you soothe, comfort, and cherish me. As I face my fears, help me become an emblem of your healing, a quiet presence along the way, one who comforts others with your presence. Amen.

I Will Make a Pathway for You

MY CHILD, I AM WITH YOU WHEN YOU ARE CAUGHT UP IN DESTRUCTIVE PATTERNS, FEAR, RESENTMENT, AND ISOLATION. When you are facing behavior and things in your life you cannot change by yourself, you can call to me. I am the higher power who will give you aid when no aid seems possible. I come to you through my word spoken through the Scriptures, and finally in my love made touchable and manifest in my incarnation. My love for you is shown in the breaking of the bread and the drinking of the wine as you taste me bodily. In the crucifix you view my broken body. Through my brokenness I heal your brokeness. When you anguish and are in deep despair, if you come to me, I will lift you up. When there seems no pathway ahead, I will make a pathway for you. My love for you is like the Father's love: strong, firm, and gentle with the gentleness that only parents can feel.

I love you in your anguish. I love you in the joyful times, too, for I am a God of dancing and joy. Take delight in me just as you delight in an infant or a sunset or a mountain or an ocean. My love can even conquer the dread of death. As I was raised from the dead, so can you be raised from that fear of death, fear of death for yourself and for others.

After a dull winter, spring comes. I am the one who brings springtime to your life. When you feel most alone, I am nearest to you. Call on me. Call on my name. Touch the cloak of my garment, for I will never abandon you. I will never leave you. I will never let you go.

SCRIPTURE

Do not fear: I am with you; do not be anxious: I am your God. I will strengthen you, I will help you, I will uphold you with my victorious right hand. ✢ Isaiah 41:10

PRAYER

Jesus, I continue the steps of my journey. Guide my thoughts. Help me see more clearly the contours of my soul, the patterns of my thoughts. Help me touch this moment and give it to you, so that you may flood me with your love and show me the seeds of eternity hidden in the ordinary things. Amen.

Take Delight in Me in Times of Need

MY CHILD, WHEN YOU CONFRONT LOSSES AND TRANSITIONS IN YOUR LIFE that you cannot change by yourself, you can call to me. I am the higher power who will give you aid when no aid seems possible. My devotion to you is made touchable in my incarnation. Take delight in me, just as you delight in an infant or a sunset or a mountain or an ocean. You can delight in me.

My friendship can even conquer the dread of death. As I was raised from the dead, so can you be raised from that fear of death for yourself and for those you hold dear. After winter comes spring. Shoots of green come up from the earth, flowers blossom, and trees fill out brilliantly with green leaves. I bring springtime to you. When life becomes bleak and cold, through my presence, through the warmth and enormity of my love, I can bring springtime. When you feel most alone, I am closest to you. Call on me. Call on my name. Touch the cloak of my garment, for I will never forsake you. I will never leave you. I will never let you go. Hold on to me.

My love is like a reunion. Reunions can be joyous times— meeting old classmates, reconnecting with people from your youth, going back to the house you grew up in. When you call on me, you feel the brightness of reunion. My love is rest. After a prolonged period of exercise, I am the rest that comes when you finish. I am the rest that comes to you after toil and labor. I am the God who enables and guides you.

SCRIPTURE
He will wipe every tear from their eyes, and there shall be no more death or mourning, wailing or pain, for the old order has passed away. ✛ **REVELATION 21:4**

PRAYER
Dear Lord, when I have difficulties I cannot change by myself, may the warm hearth of your friendship change how I see the world. When I need an about-face in life, remind me to seek your help. Amen.

I Can Relieve Your Anxiety and Stress

My child, as a mother delights in placing a child on her lap so as to feed and caress him, as a father kneels before a bed with a child, teaching her the Our Father, so I delight to treat you with the same tenderness, calm, and nurturing when the worries and stresses of this world overtake you.

I promise you rest. "Come to me all you who are tired and heavy laden, and I will give you rest," as I said in the Gospel of Matthew. Come to me. Lay your burdens at my feet and I can console you with the peace that only I can bring.

Stress comes from many different sources: the pain of the past, the anxieties of the present, and the fears of the future. Also, the lack of a firm connection with me can lead to heavy stress. You were created bodily for connection with me, and you suffer in both body and soul when that connection becomes impaired. Take time to pray each day, taking a sunbath in my love, resting in my Presence. Read calming Scripture, especially the psalms that speak of distress and God's comfort in the midst of distress. Frequent the sacrament of reconciliation, make daily acts of contrition, and relish the depths of my mercy, which sets you free.

I want to cradle you, embrace you, and surround you with the light of my resurrection, which can melt all fear, worry, and stress for eternity. Reach out to me. I take your hands, and you can feel the healing warmth pass from my hands to yours, passing through your arms into your soul, bringing the peace that surpasses understanding.

I knew stress and worry on this earth, but I also knew the Father's comfort. And you can know comfort too.

SCRIPTURE
"Peace I leave with you; my peace I give to you. Not as the world gives do I give it to you. Do not let your hearts be troubled or afraid." ✝ JOHN 14:27

PRAYER
Dear Lord, sometimes life feels so stressful. I feel so worn down by the pressures every day seems to bring. Please help me to root myself in prayer and Scripture, to feel your peace even in the midst of the stress and chaos. Amen.

Tell Me of Your Sorrows

My child, in Scripture I call out to you; I want to be your friend; I want to heal the bruised places within. Scripture is the story of my love of my people Israel, how I separated them, made them my unique people, delivered them from slavery, and guided them as they became a nation. You touch me in the psalms that cry out to me for help, for I want you to cry out to me when you hurt, not just when you are joyful and want to praise. It is also said of me that I had my own sorrows, appointed with grief in the sorrow. Take my hand and place it on your chest to heal your wounds in your heart. Tell me of your sorrows.

Call out to me. Do not keep it within. Do not harbor your hurt within but reach out to me. Scream, yell, whatever, because the psalmist screamed and yelled and cried out to me and I will always be faithful.

I touch you in the stories about me. I let you walk with me on the path that I have walked. I know this is a lot to begin with, but I cannot hold silent in reaching out to you with my love, in reaching out to you with my comfort and healing.

SCRIPTURE

Out of the depths I call to you, Lord;
    Lord, hear my cry!
May your ears be attentive
    to my cry for mercy.
✝ PSALM 130:1–2

PRAYER

Lord, I want to call out to you in my pain and suffering. Help me to trust that you want to know everything about me, even the parts of me that hurt and that I am ashamed of. Help me to reach out to you. Amen.

When You Feel Deserted, I Can Be There with You

MY CHILD, I AM PRESENT WHETHER YOUR SENSES ARE AWARE OF ME OR NOT. In times of tragedy and misunderstanding, I am far closer to you than you may realize. When you feel absent, when you feel deserted, I am right there.

I knew times when I felt deserted too—in the Garden of Gethsemane, when my disciples did not truly understand who I was, and when I was met with the cold hatred of the religious elite who could not understand that my miracles pointed to a God of love. What happens in those times in which you feel abandoned? This is what I hope happens for you: that you cry out, that you storm heaven, that you wave your fist at me if you need to, that you let your voice cry out, "Help me, Lord. Oh, help me, Lord."

Pouring out your desperation, your loneliness, your insecurities to me at a time when you are not feeling consoled is among the greatest acts of faith you can ever engage in. Turning to me when things seem dark or dim around you draws me like flower blossoms draw bees. When you take time for me in the quiet, I can do marvelous things for your soul. I can sing a song so beautiful in your soul that it lasts into eternity. I can drown you in the light of my glory, splendor, and majesty. I can so amaze with the vividness of my nearness that you know you have been embraced by the everlasting.

Seek me in prayer; seek me in Scripture. Behind Scripture lies an eternity of wisdom and grace. Treat the Scripture almost like words of love, whispering quiet passages to yourself as a husband would whisper sweet nothings into his wife's ear or a wife her husband. Continue with me in prayer and you will feel my holy fire in your bones. All this is calling you to an experience beyond your ability to articulate it. All this is calling you to a plunge into the depths of my heart. So take time for me in silence, in Scripture, and in right relationships with one another, and I can carry you further and longer and deeper into the mystery of my presence, into the mystery that created all that is.

SCRIPTURE

And about three o'clock Jesus cried out in a loud voice, *"Eli, Eli, lema sabachthani?"* which means, *"My God, my God, why have you forsaken me?"* ✢ **Matthew 27:46**

PRAYER

Dear Lord, there are times when you seem so far away. There are times when I feel abandoned. Help me to remember even in those dark hours that you are always with me. Help me to cry out to you, to trust in your presence and love. Amen.

I Can Ease and Untie the Tangles of the Past

MY CHILD, THE TYPE OF PRAYER I CALL YOU TO—RESTING IN THE LAP OF MY LOVE, BATHING IN MY LOVE—CAN TRANSFIGURE YOUR WHOLE LIFE. To truly capture the fresh newness the Scriptures talk about, allow me into the deeper levels of your heart. The warmth of my consolation gives such safety that the tangles inside of you ease up, untie, and let go when surrounded by caring and nurture strong enough to replace the hurt. This is the kind of love I offer you. The tenderness I express deep within you can so soothe the inward parts of you that clutch so tightly to the tangles of the past, allowing you to give your heart over into my hands. Then, a brand-new day can begin.

This call to quiet is not hard or complex. It is letting the Spirit pray through you with sighs too deep for words. Each of you is a fathomless depth and only I can know you fully. In quiet prayer and meditation, you give the Holy Spirit permission to search your depths. As your healing unfolds, you may find that at times a hurt is welling up inside of you and you do not know why. When that happens, you can grieve and weep and let go of your grip, surrendering your insides to my curing hands. This is what St. Paul meant by sighs too deep for words.

Over a period of time, as prayer deepens the work of healing within you, a deep joy will root itself in the wellsprings of your being. The sunshine will appear to have more splendor, and you will be able to feel the warmth of words expressed by others rather than suspect ill will hidden in them. You will learn to drink in the beauty of each present moment. The trees, the stars and blue hills, the touch of another human being will appear to you as symbols aching with a meaning that can never be voiced in words. Nature begins to mirror the eternal. Water does more than wash you; it brightens your heart. The earth you walk on does more than hold our bodies; it gladdens your entire being, transmitting to your being the tenderness that is my heart.

SCRIPTURE
The Spirit too comes to the aid of our weakness; for we do not know how to pray as we ought, but the Spirit itself intercedes with inexpressible groanings. And the one who searches hearts knows what is the intention of the Spirit, because it intercedes for the holy ones according to God's will. ✝ **ROMANS 8:26–27**

PRAYER

Dear Lord, sometimes I do not know how to pray. I don't know how to call out to you in my time of darkness and despair. I don't know how to let go of the pain that is deep within me. Please come to me, hear my inexpressible groanings, and shed your light on the dark parts of my soul. Please heal the pain and woundedness so that I may fully appreciate your glory. Amen.

Reflection Questions

It is in the midst of our pain and suffering that it is easiest to feel that God has abandoned us. We cry out and hear nothing but silence, but those are the times when we need to lean on the Lord the most. Can you trust that God is with you even in those times when you feel most alone? Can you turn to him in prayer and trust in God's answer even when things don't turn out the way you want them to?

Look back at your life. When was a time that you felt that God had deserted you? With the benefit of hindsight, is there any good that came out of that painful situation? God can bring good even out of the worst circumstances. Is it possible that he is working in your life in ways that you don't see or understand at the moment?

Who do you know who is hurting? What can you do to help them? How can you bring the peace and love of Jesus to that person?

What burdens are you carrying today? Imagine laying them at the foot of the cross or handing them over to Jesus. Resist the urge to pick them back up again. How does that feel?

Feel Amazement *in the* Lord's Presence

Stand in Amazement

MY CHILD, ONE OF THE GREATEST GIFTS I GIVE YOU IS THE GIFT OF STANDING IN SILENT AMAZEMENT at my presence in the world, deep silent amazement at my spectacular creation, which reflects my splendor. Look up at the stars in the sky and you get a glimpse of my forever. Allowing me to astound you is perhaps the greatest prayer gift of all.

Throughout the history of the Church, holy women and men have sought the gift of tears to express the silent amazement. When your face is watered with tears of the eternal loveliness that is my presence, you have passed from death to life.

You can come to be amazed in me in the writings of Scripture and let them train your heart.

Please love me, not just for the gifts I give you, but for the heart I show to you, a heart that gives itself away. Love those who are not easy to love. Go out of yourself; lose yourself for my kingdom. As I said in Scripture: "If any wants to become my followers, let them deny themselves, and take up their crosses and follow me" (Matthew 16:24).

During the days of my life on earth, there were times that I yearned to simply return to Nazareth and live a simple life. There were times I wanted to retreat from people wanting me to help them. I experienced disappointments, too—those who did not understand my words, those who failed me in not understanding my mission. My very disciples failed me. There were times I wanted to retreat from all this and live a quiet, normal life. Yet I persisted. It took lots of prayer and communion with the Father and study of Scripture. I had to go out of my heart. It was not easy. In short, I bore the burden of the cross, not just in my final execution, but throughout my life. Yet all that is the cross ripened into resurrection. Take up your crosses and you will find them ripen too, in time, into unspeakable glory, the ultimate amazement.

SCRIPTURE
Then he said to all, "If anyone wishes to come after me, he must deny himself and take up his cross daily and follow me. For whoever wishes to save his life will lose it, but whoever loses his life for my sake will save it." ✛ **Luke 9:23–24**

PRAYER
Dear Jesus, help me celebrate the joy and honestly face the sorrow. Open my eyes so that I can see your footsteps and interventions throughout my life's journey. Help me see my story as a story of redemption. Enfold me in your tenderness as I look at the pain. May the healing that comes to me bring me new strength to love and serve your people and your world. As I heal, enable me to help others heal. Amen.

To Hold on to Me Is to Have Fire in Your Bones

MY CHILD, WHEN YOUR HOUSEHOLD LIGHTS GO OFF DUE TO A LOSS OF ELECTRICITY AND YOUR HOUSE DARKENS, you need a larger light—the light of the sun. You throw open the drapes and let the sunlight burst in. When the light in your hearts grows dim, you can look to a greater light—the everlasting light I bring—and let it burst in your heart. Soak in that light. When your heart grows dim due to turmoil and events beyond your control, you can turn to the one light that always brightens—the light I bring.

Resist the urge to set your heart's affections on changeable things when you can cling to the one light. You need the burst of the light that John said came into the world. You need me: uncreated and eternal light. As the Scriptures say, "While you have the light, believe in the light that you may be children of the light" (John 12:36). The real heart of my glory and my light is my love reflected in my humanity. Instead of putting your trust in what is changeable, bathe in the sunrays of my presence.

To hold on to me is to have fire in your bones. Your eyes could not bear the whole splendor of the center of the sun or even of its surface. So it is with the splendor of the light that is everlasting. To look directly at it is too much for your eyes to bear, but if you want to see the splendor, you can simply see this eternal glory in my caring face, my utterly human face.

SCRIPTURE
"I am the light of the world. Whoever follows me will not walk in darkness, but will have the light of life."
✝ JOHN 8:12

PRAYER
Merciful and loving God, may the Light of your Presence brighten me, body and soul. You are nearer than my heartbeat, closer than my breath. Help me in my remembering, for you are the holder of my steps and the keeper of my story. You remember when I forget. May I see more clearly how you guided me in all the turnings and windings of my life. May your love be a light along my path. Amen.

Experience the Fullness of Eternity

MY CHILD, I WISH FOR YOU TO KNOW AND EXPERIENCE THE FULL-
NESS OF ETERNITY. You do not have to wait till after your death to experience eternal life. It is a property of life that can burst in on you right now and then go on forever.

I can so charge up your world that you will see the ordinary things—the smell of rain on the sidewalk, a brisk wind on your face, beautiful sunlight coming down, or just daily living—enchanted with wonder. A loaf of bread can remind you that I gave myself as bread that is broken that invites you even now into the never-ending banquet, the everlasting Eucharist. Daily encounters with people can take on a profundity drenched in immortality. The rhythm of your words, the humanity of your touch and voice, can carry a hint of the ceaseless. I can fill the crevices of your soul with a rich, never-ending mystery.

How? How does all this come about? Through prayer, sharing spirituality with others, Scripture, and the Eucharist—in short, faith. Faith in me is not so much believing the hard to believe; rather, it is opening wide the windows of your heart to the sunrays of my love that beat down upon you. My eternity can so make over your world that the stuff of daily living is charmed with a holy delight. It does not mean that there will not be hard times or sorrowful times or times of misunderstanding with others. It does not mean that you will be forever free of tragedy. What it does mean is that taking time for me bathes your world with a mystery that is ceaseless.

SCRIPTURE
Praise the Lord from the heavens;
    praise him in the heights.
Praise him, all you his angels;
    give praise, all you his hosts.
Praise him, sun and moon.
Let them all praise the Lord's name;
    for he commanded and they were created.
✠ PSALM 148:1–3, 5

PRAYER
Dear Lord, open my eyes so that I may see you in the everyday miracles that surround me. Help me to witness your mystery and to share that wonder with others. Help me to have faith and to trust in you always, even in the hard times. May I always be amazed by all the wondrous gifts you have given me. Amen.

Heaven Is Rushing toward You

My child, I promised you I would have a place, a mansion, prepared for you when I called you home. Heaven is not strange, wild, unlike earth, but rather it is earth living as I would have it live. My child, glory is coming. The new creation, the new Jerusalem, heaven, is rushing toward you. Heaven is not streets paved with gold or houses roofed with diamonds. Instead, it is like those moments in your lifetime when you battled in a relationship until a time came when you both forgave the other and you both felt God's arms encircle you. It is like when you turned from injurious patterns and asked God's aid to help you with behavior you could no longer handle yourself, perhaps a struggle with alcohol, drugs, or other addictions. In those instances of desperation, God entered into your hurt and you felt heaven. Heaven is a place where your hurts and addictions no longer burden you. Heaven is the place where sin no longer weighs you down, for I have profoundly forgiven your sins. It is in the enlightened moments of everyday reality that you taste the everlasting. It is the restoration of this earth, this world, and of glory shining upon the ordinary so that it sparkles with a divine presence.

Heaven is the ordinariness of our lives transfigured. Pebbles in a clear brook will show sunshine on them. The water in which they are sunk glorifies and magnifies them. If you looked at the little bits of stone lying beneath the ripples of the brook, you would see they are jewels. Cast the everydayness of your life into that great stream and the little things in your life will turn wondrous both now and forever.

SCRIPTURE
"In my Father's house there are many dwelling places. If there were not, would I have told you that I am going to prepare a place for you? And if I go and prepare a place for you, I will come back again and take you to myself, so that where I am you also may be." ✛ JOHN 14:2–3

PRAYER
Lord, help me to see heaven showing up in the little things of this life. May the immediacy of your presence here and now remind me of your nearness into eternity. Amen.

I Can Infuse You with Wonder

My child, I stand ready to take your hand, to infuse you with a wonder, a joy that makes earthly things and earthly memories pure and touched by the amazement of eternity. It is in the stuff of daily life transfixed and transformed that heaven will come to be. I can eternally redeem what was lost and put together what was missing. Glory, heaven— the new creation is like seeing again through the eyes of the toddler when everything is utterly fascinating, utterly fresh, and capable of communicating the presence of the light that transforms the ordinary into the holy.

My child, see with new eyes. See the depth and the freshness of each smile you see, of each smell you smell, of each taste you taste. Taste the inherent glory that is in those things, for I have given you eyes that can see wonder. I have given you eyes that can turn the world into one great astonishment. Have you ever driven in the midst of very high mountains with the mist all around them and heard the scene before you, as it were, express mystery and eternity, aching with the beauty that words cannot express? Heaven is life turned into that beauty, real human life as real and earthly as an unconsecrated host and wine, which are consecrated by glory and become the wondrous drink and meal of the resurrection. Abandon yourself to me and I will give you a taste of glory.

In many ways the new creation, heaven, glory, is like a beautiful tapestry. If you look on the back side of a tapestry, all you see are different colored dangling strings in no particular order. That's how your lives are. They are tied and knotted up. They are somewhat incoherent at times. The pattern is not readily visible. But if you reverse it and look at the front, you see the beautiful picture depicted by the tapestry. Right now, you see the struggles and the disconnectedness. You see the loose strings. But, in eternity, the tapestry will be turned over and you will see the front and see how it looks from my eyes and see the beautifully woven tapestry forever dwelling in the timelessness of my eternity.

SCRIPTURE
Let the heavens be glad and the earth rejoice;
    let the sea and what fills it resound;
    let the plains be joyful and all that is in them.
Then let all the trees of the forest rejoice
    before the Lord who comes to govern the earth,
To govern the world with justice
    and the peoples with faithfulness.
✢ PSALMS 96:11–13

PRAYER

Dear Jesus, help me to see the beauty and the glory in your creation. Help me to always trust that you are weaving a beautiful tapestry in my life, even when I can only see the tangled threads. Amen.

I Can Transform Earthiness into Heavenly Joy

MY CHILD, THE WEDDING FEAST AT CANA WAS FULL OF HUMAN PLEASURE: good food, good wine, and good company. Is there room for pleasure and fun in the joyful wonder I can bring? My very first miracle in the Gospel of John was to change jars of water into jars of premium wine, to take what is part of human fun and infuse it with awe. By changing water into wine, I changed human fun into heavenly joy. I can heighten human pleasure and the plain fun humans can have into a godly delight. I made the fun and pleasure of a wedding party into something wondrous.

Just like a taper plunged into a vat of oxygen bursts out in brightness, so can your earthly pleasures blaze brightly when you invite me in. A scene in nature at its best and highest, without me, is like some fine landscape in the evening shadow; but when you bring me into it, it is as though the bright sun lights on it and it sparkles from every bend of the moving river, brings beauty into that which was shady, opens all the flowering petals, and sets all the birds singing in the sky. The whole scene changes when a beam of light from me falls upon earthly joys. When my Presence is a part of it, when you invite me in, the beauty shines with eternal loveliness.

I who transform the water of earthly gladness into the wine of heavenly blessedness can do the same thing for the bitter waters of sorrow and can make them the occasions of solemn joy. In changing water into wine at the wedding banquet in Cana, I showed myself to be a heightener of earthly joys and fun. I demonstrated my willingness to pour everlasting and pure joy into weary, thirsty hearts.

SCRIPTURE
When the headwaiter tasted the water that had become wine, without knowing where it came from (although the servers who had drawn the water knew), the headwaiter called the bridegroom and said to him, "Everyone serves good wine first, and then when people have drunk freely, an inferior one; but you have kept the good wine until now."
✝ JOHN 2:9–10

PRAYER
Dear Jesus, you are the source of all true lasting joy. Give me the gift of wonder that I may fully appreciate the beauty of your creation all around me. Allow me to always feel your presence. Amen.

I Am the Gateway to Joy

My child, I am the gateway into immense joy. Joy is the deep-down sense of well-being and fullness that comes when you draw close to me. It affects you totally, body as well as soul. Wonder and joy are often used interchangeably in the Scripture. When the Father, Holy Spirit, and I flood you, the world becomes fresh and new.

Joy and wonder defy logical definition. They are felt more than defined. Joy is a part of my very being. Joy is a fruit of the Spirit.

Part of joy means grieving in prayer when we need to grieve, learning the lessons you need to learn, taking all of your emotions and laying them at my feet, so the Spirit can transfigure them.

It is a mistake to think that joy comes only when things are going well for you. It can be harder to open up to joy when sorrow comes, when you are reeling from the news that you have been laid off from the job that supported your family for thirty years, hurting from the loss of a lifelong friend who stops speaking to you, seemingly without reason, or standing by the graveside of a loved one as the priest or deacon recites the final prayers.

The good news I bring is that even when you encounter sorrow or feel lost because life has pulled the rug from beneath your feet, you can still experience joy.

How can faith help you in the midst of these sorrows? I assure you that even in your sorrows you can find joy, genuine joy. This is no fake joy in which you soft-pedal and deny the harsh realities of life, plastering on a syrupy smile and saying, "Now let's all just be happy." Rather, it is the summons from me to pause and acknowledge my presence, to take to heart Paul's admonition to "rejoice, again I say rejoice" (Phil 4:4). In choosing joy at every stage of your life—in the low periods of life as well as in the highs—you acknowledge your total dependence on God and my unfailing love. You may indeed walk through the valley of the shadow of death, but you can take comfort that it is only a shadow. Sorrow can bring joy when it leads you to cling to me, the source of all joy.

SCRIPTURE

Even though I walk through the valley of the shadow
 of death,
I will feel no evil, for you are with me;
 your rod and your staff comfort me.
You set a table before me in front of my enemies;
 You anoint my head with oil; my cup overflows.
Indeed, goodness and mercy will pursue me all the days
 of my life;
 I will dwell in the house of the Lord for endless days.
✝ Psalm 23:4–6

PRAYER

Dear Lord, I want the joy you offer. I want to feel your presence even in the times when my heart feels as if it might break from sorrow. I believe that true joy and peace can only be found in you. Help me to always cling to you. Amen.

Allow Me to Lead You

My child, I am able to enflame your whole person with my Presence. There is no need to fear. Just draw me in and my flame will make all things new. My love is a devouring flame. You could call me beauty, and many have, and that is true of me. You could call me purity, and many have, and that is true of me. People may call me truth. People may call me strength. All those would be true. Calling me light is another beautiful thing to do. Calling me love is the profoundest truth of all because that resonates with my heart.

I am limitless love, limitless compassion, limitless caring, and I embrace your soul. Open up to me. Allow me to embrace you. I am love that does not cease. I am love that wins out in the end. I am like a hurricane, a tsunami wave that pushes away everything that opposes it. My love has a power to make passageways for your life and passageways for your heart. I am asking you to follow me, and I vow that this love will lead you. This is not a new idea. This is an old idea manifested and made perfect in my incarnation. I am like the sun. I am the kind of sun that has no twilight or evening. It shines on and on for eternity, showering beauty and color and light on everything in its path.

You are able to come toward me because I come toward you.

SCRIPTURE

God is light, and in him there is no darkness at all.

✝ 1 John 1:5

PRAYER

Dear Jesus, you are light, you are truth, you are strength, and you are love. I praise you for all that you are. I praise you for the light you shine on my path and for the love you give to me. Help me to always follow you wherever you lead me. Amen.

Reflection Questions

Wonder, the ability to be amazed, is one of God's greatest gifts. What is a moment in your life when you felt the gift of wonder? Perhaps it was a beautiful moment in nature or holding a newborn baby for the first time. Whatever it was, take the time to thank God for that gift.

Do you think it is possible to make a conscious effort to add more wonder to your life? Go out for a walk or simply sit in nature. Take time to really look at the gifts God has given us in creation. Marvel at the beauty of a flower or the complexity of a simple insect or the fact that a huge tree grew from a small seed. What does creation reveal about the power of God?

Do you take time to appreciate the everyday miracles of your life? Take a few moments to sit in quiet and pay attention to your breath. Breathe in and out. Feel your heart beating. Each of us (despite whatever health problems we might be facing) is a beautiful and complex work of God's creation. Our very lives are a miracle. How would your life look different if you took time to marvel at the miracles you encounter every day?

What do you imagine heaven is like? What is the most awe-inspiring moment you have ever had in your life? What would it be like to experience that on an eternal basis? Can you bring a bit of eternal life into your daily life? Can you take time to simply rest in God?

For decades, **Deacon Eddie Ensley** and **Deacon Robert Herrmann** have offered parish missions, retreats, and conferences throughout the country, drawing whole parishes together and recharging congregations. People are reconciled. Faith is awakened. Vocations are discovered. Here is what one pastor had to say about the event the deacons held at his parish:

> "The mission proved to be a tremendous help for our families....Our attendance was better than ever. The guided meditations throughout were vivid and uplifting. The parish mission was filled with solid content. The greatest compliment has been in the attendance." *(Father John T. Euker, St. John the Baptist Parish, Perryopolis, Pennsylvania)*

Would you like to invite the authors to your parish mission, retreat, or conference? The deacons can also lead retreats for deacons as well as religious education conferences. To bring them to your parish or your event or to ask for an information and to view a video of a parish mission and receive a packet about what their retreats and conferences can offer your area, you can **visit their website www.parishmission.net**, or email Deacon Ensley at **pmissions@charter.net**.